HOW TO BE Y
HUSBAN

D0204617

❧ Best Friend ❧
365
WAYS TO EXPRESS YOUR LOVE

CAY BOLIN & CINDY TRENT

PIÑON PRESS

P.O. Box 35007, Colorado Springs, Colorado 80935

Library of Congress Catalog Card Number: 94-69197
ISBN 08910-98747

Printed in the United States of America

1 2 3 4 5 6 7 8 9 10 11 12 13 14 15 / 99 98 97 96 95

To our best friends, Dan and John,
who believe in us,
who encourage us to do what we think is impossible,
and who love us no matter what

INTRODUCTION

It was Thursday, the last day of school. As I took our eight-year-old to her classroom down the hall, I noticed the lack of excitement and chaos typically associated with the end of the school year. A mother came up to me and asked if I had heard about Nicolas' dad. He had died in the middle of the night of a heart attack—a forty-four-year-old father of a second-grade son and fifth-grade daughter and the husband of Ann. I couldn't believe the news. Charlie had been at school on Tuesday for the awards ceremony. He had been at Nicholas' five-pitch baseball game on Wednesday.

Several weeks after Charlie's death I ran into Ann at the baseball field. She began to relay to me how they were coping with their loss. She was somewhat overwhelmed with the many decisions that she alone had to make. Then she shared these words, "I wish Charlie were here to help me make the decisions that will affect the life of our family. He was my husband and the father of my children but most importantly he was my very best friend." Ann experienced a double loss—the loss of her husband and her best friend.

Husbands and wives don't always see each other as best friends. Our daughter Haley's best friend moved to Houston recently. When they said their goodbyes, Haley gave Courtney a necklace with half of a heart on it. Haley kept the other half. The two parts of the heart fit together to make one complete heart inscribed with the words, "Best Friends."

Does your heart fit together with the heart of your husband? Are the words "Best Friends" inscribed on it?

What does it take to be best friends with your husband? What barriers must be crossed?

Busyness—There are many demands on our time . . . children, work, community involvement. Do we have anything left for our husband? So often I think he will understand. But husbands need to know they are special to us. There are many little ways to show this. Often I just need to be reminded to refocus on my husband. As my pastor reminded me, it seems that the ones closest to me suffer the most from my busyness. Busyness takes more than it gives.

Expectations—We begin marriage with unspoken desires that we "expect" our husbands to fulfill. During premarital counseling Dan and I talked about some of our expectations. My dad had always taken out the garbage, and I assumed that Dan would do the same. However at his house, taking out the garbage was done by his mom. On the first night of our honeymoon I expected Dan to wear pajamas. He didn't even own a pair. To meet that expectation he bought a pair of very ugly olive green pajamas (which became a tradition to pass on to each of his brothers as they married).

When our premarital counselor asked me what I would do to honor Dan, I didn't hesitate to say that I would prepare an elegant candlelight dinner complete with fresh flowers and china. Our counselor inquired of Dan if this would honor him. "I would enjoy that," he said, "but there are other ways to honor me." I was surprised. If Dan had prepared a meal for me or taken me out to a nice restaurant, I would have been honored.

For the first seventeen years of marriage I baked homemade cakes for Dan's birthday. On his forty-first birthday he said that he would prefer a bakery cake. Growing up he'd had homemade cakes and had always wanted store-bought cakes. Growing up I had always had store-bought cakes and had wanted homemade ones. We were unaware of our different expectations until we discussed them. Consequently, we have spent many hours during more than eighteen years of marriage expressing our expectations.

Little things—We joke about the little things that cause conflict in marriage . . . not putting the cap on the toothpaste tube, leaving the toilet seat up, chewing ice, belching at the table (and other such noises). It is easy to focus on the little annoying things that take away from a husband-wife relationship rather than focusing on what makes husbands and wives best friends.

When Dan and I begin to focus on the little things, we make fun pacts. No matter what goes wrong we have fun . . . like the evening I was grilling chicken for sixteen guests at our July Fourth party when the propane that fueled the grill ran out, or the time we had spent thousands of dollars on a new mini van and it quit running on the way home from the dealership. At moments like these you can watch your friendship dissolve or in our case make fun pacts determining you'll be friends no matter what happens.

Dan and I have faced other barriers as well. Shortly before our ninth year of marriage our four-year-old daughter was diagnosed with leukemia. We spent five years living on the edge as our daughter went through chemotherapy, a bone marrow transplant, and finally death. Our natural tendency was to pour all that we had into our two children, leaving nothing for each other. We knew our days with Catie were numbered. It was difficult not to spend every moment with her.

Because of some wise counsel from friends whose child had been born with a disabling disease, Dan and I began going on a date one evening a week (a tradition that we have continued). We had been told that the divorce rate between husbands and wives who have a child facing a terminal illness greatly increases over the national average. Of couples who have had a child die, 70 percent are divorced or separated in the first year after death. Ninety percent of these couples are divorced in the second year.

What holds marriages together in the midst of busyness, differing expectations, the little annoyances as well as the major crisis? I believe one essential element is friendship. This book is full of ideas on how you can become your husband's best friend.

—CAY BOLIN

1

Drop everything and go out to lunch
with him on a weekday.

2

Don't over commit yourself.
Leave time for him.

3

When you think he is lost, let him wander around as long as he wants until he decides to stop and ask for directions.

4

Leave a note under his pillow.

5

When he goes out of town,
pack chocolate chip cookies in his suitcase.

6

Always keep at least two days of clean clothes
in the closet.

7
Plan a candlelight dinner for the two of you
(after the kids have gone to bed).

8
Let him use the TV remote control,
without complaining.

9
Develop a common interest.

10
Surprise him by getting a baby sitter
for an evening out.

11
Listen to his dreams
without telling him
they will never come true.

❖

12
If he had "store-bought" birthday cakes as a boy,
give him a home-baked one.
If he had "homemade" cakes, get him a store-
bought cake for his next birthday.

13
When you drive his car and change radio stations, set it back on his favorite station.

14
Ride in the cart with him when he plays golf.

15
Write him a poem for his birthday.

16
Try not to interrupt during the crucial parts
of a televised ball game.

17
Tell him when his zipper is down.

18
Write him a letter and send it to his work place.

19
Agree together on a budget
and make sure you stay within it.

20
Meet him at the door with a kiss
when he comes home from work.

21
Window shop together.

22
Make him a meal he enjoys
even if it is not your favorite.

23
Go on a business trip with him.

24

When your schedule allows, take an afternoon nap
so you are rested when he comes home from work.

25

Give him private lessons as a gift.
(Golf, tennis, guitar, fly-fishing, etc.)

26

Make him a Valentine's Day card.

27

Let him eat his whole dessert.
Don't say you don't care for any, then eat his.

28

Give him a stocking at Christmas
full of his favorite little things.

29
Keep a supply of his favorite cold drinks
in the refrigerator.

❖

30
If your anniversary is at a busy time of the year,
celebrate it when things slow down.

31
Have homemade cookies and milk
waiting for him when he returns home
after working late.

32
Take a class together at a community college.

33
Hold his hand when you are together.

34
Get him an instructional video
about his favorite pastime.

35
Get up with him
when he has early morning meetings,
no matter how early it is. After he is gone
you can go back to bed.

36
Listen to classical music together.

───────◈───────

37
When someone asks him a question,
never answer for him.

───────◈───────

38
Discover what pleases him and do it.

39

Pick up his clothes from the cleaners
before it closes for the weekend.

40

Take the initiative to mow the yard
once in a while when his life is hectic.

41

Learn about one of his interests.

42
Go to a school board meeting together.

43
Work together
to elect a government official.

44

Read a book aloud to each other.

✦

45

Notice any missing buttons on his shirts
and sew them on before he mentions it.

46

Give him some time to unwind
when he first comes home from work.

47

Give him your undivided attention
for a period of time each evening
(after the children go to bed).

48
Keep yourself in shape.

◈

49
Stay up until he gets home
from a long, late trip.

50
Ask him about his day
before you tell him about yours.

———————⬧———————

51
Love your children.

52
Keep plenty of his favorite food or snacks
in the pantry.

53
Put an encouraging note
in his lunch.

54

Laugh together.

55

Always check with him
before you throw away any of his junky looking
important papers.

56
Say, "I'm sorry."

57
Have extra food on hand
in case he invites guests home for dinner
unexpectedly.

58

Call him at work
to let him know you are
thinking of him.

59

For his birthday, make a donation
to his favorite charity.

60
Match his socks.

61
Look at your wedding pictures together.

62
Cry together.

63
Encourage him to do things with the guys.

64
Together return to the spot where
he asked you to marry him.

65

When he has a day off,
let him have it
without a list of things you need done.

66

Don't be his mother.

67

Build a fire in the fireplace some evening
before he comes home from work.

68

Read the headlines of the sports page
so that you'll know who won the "big game."

69

Use the nice china
even when you don't have company.

70

Have your picture taken together
in a photo booth.

71

Learn a foreign language together.

❖

72

When he has a day off,
let it be one without having
to supervise the kids.

73

Pack his bags before a business trip.

❖

74

Listen to the tape or watch the video
of your wedding.

75

Keep one area of your home
clean enough for company so that he can feel
free to bring home guests unexpectedly.

───────◆───────

76

Never say "I told you so."

77
Avoid interrupting during the televised news
while the scores are being given.

78
Go to your state
or county fair together.

79

Share his good qualities
when talking with others about him.

80

Carry a picture of him
in your wallet.

81
Tell your children
about your first date with him.

82
When he shops with you at the mall,
make sure not to stay too long.

83
Subscribe to a sports magazine for him
and read it once in a while.

84
Screen his phone calls at home.
Ask him ahead of time
which calls he wants to accept.

85
Sleep like two spoons in a drawer.

86
Put up a hammock in the backyard
for him to enjoy.

87

Go to a foreign country together and volunteer
for a humanitarian cause.

88

Play a computer game with him.

89
Go camping with him and enjoy it.

90
Sometimes go to bed
before the evening news
and spend that time talking.

91
Join a growth group with other couples.

92
Plant a garden together.

93
Place an ad in the newspaper
to announce his birthday.

94
Go outside in the evening
and gaze at the stars.

95
Cook a meal together for friends.

96
See your doctor regularly.

97
Go on a date and talk about each other
(not the kids).

98
Buy him sun screen
and encourage him to use it
to protect his skin from the sun.

99
Run a "Fun Run" together.

100
Invite his family over for a meal.

101
Wear your hair the way he likes it.

102
Subtract the checks in the checkbook ledger.

103
Laugh at his jokes.

104
Go to a car dealership after hours
and dream together about a new car.

105
Volunteer with him at a local charity.

106
Listen to record albums or cassettes
from your college days
and reminisce together.

107
Stop at historical markers.

108
Give him the cherry
off the top of your banana split.

109
On your anniversary write him a letter
telling him why you love him.

110

Never criticize his family.

111

Read a book about how to improve
your marriage.

112

Whisper a secret in his ear.

113
Stand aside while he assembles his new "toy,"
without suggesting
that he read the instructions.

114
Cook on the healthy side.

115
When he gives you a gift of clothing, wear it.

116
Leave him an encouraging message on the answering machine.

117

Go to a weekend
marriage enrichment
conference together.

118

Be on time.

119
Replace borrowed change
out of the change holder in his car.

120
Fall asleep together listening to a baseball game
on the radio.

121
Go out for coffee together.

122
Look at house-plan books with him,
and design a dream house.

123
Brush your teeth.

124
Look through your high school yearbooks together.

125
Go to a hardware store with him.

126
After you make up from a disagreement, bake him his favorite dessert.

127
Remember, he is not your dad.

128
When he is home, limit your time on the phone.

129
Rent the video of a movie that was popular
when you were in college.

130
Remember dates that are important to him.

131
Make his favorite jam or jelly.

132
Attend his ball games and cheer for him.

133
Listen when he explains how his computer works, even if you have little or no interest.

134
Make sure you both understand your family finances.

135

When he comes home from work,
ask him about the important meeting
or issue he was worried about
when he left that morning.

❖

136

Look your best—dress to honor him.

137
Never eat onions unless he does.

138
Save your flirting for him.

139
Have an extra set of keys made for your house
and car and hide them where they will be
available the next time he is locked out.

140
Learn the rules to his favorite sport.

141
Write him a note thanking him for the years
you have spent together.

142
When you close one of his books,
mark the place with a bookmark.

143

Videotape a special TV program
he wants to watch but will be unable to
due to a scheduling conflict.

144

Clean the garage.

145

Have something engraved on his wedding ring
for a special anniversary.

146

Wink at him from across the room
when out at a group function.

147

Tell him when his clothes don't match
before he gets dressed.

148

Tell him you think the gray hair
makes him look distinguished.

149

Give him a foot rub.

150

Have a professional portrait done
of the two of you
(without the kids).

151

Do a jigsaw puzzle together.

152
Prepare his favorite dessert
just because you love him.

153
Call your friends by name
when you and your husband meet them
even if you think he should already know
their names.

154
Rent his favorite video.

155
Go to his high school reunion
with him.

156
"People watch" together
at restaurants and airports.
Try to guess if people are married,
on first dates, leaving on a honeymoon,
or other interesting observations.

157
Discuss your expectations as a couple.

158

Display his awards and trophies.

159

Coordinate your calendars
for the month ahead.

160
Keep a scrapbook of significant events in his life.

❖

161
Never remind him
of how much weight he has gained
since your wedding
(or where he has gained it).

162
Be aware of his vision or goals and affirm them.

163
Remind yourself not to provide lessons
on table manners, especially in public.

164
Thank him for helping you
with the housework.

❖

165
Tell him you appreciate his insight and opinion
when you are making a personal decision.

166
Have a water balloon fight on a hot summer day.

167
Plan a night away for just the two of you.

168
Go fishing with him.

169
Surprise him at work
and take him to his favorite spot for lunch.

170
Tell him he looks more handsome
with less hair.

171

Never vacuum during the fourth quarter
of the ball game.

❖

172

Fix him breakfast in bed.

173
Make sure circumstances permit him
to sleep in on a Saturday morning.

174
Buy him some gadget he has always wanted
but would never buy for himself.

175
Trim his moustache.

176
Send personalized balloons to his place of work.

177
Take an evening walk together.

178
Watch his favorite sports event with him.

⊹

179
Do a few things on his "honey do" list.

⊹

180
Do a crossword puzzle together.

181
Go to a shooting range with him.

182
Share the joy of taking out the garbage.

183
Review your will together.

184
Have breakfast out on the back patio
and enjoy the morning.

185
Go biking together.

186
Clean his car.

187
Set up a war game,
using paint as ammunition,
for him and his friends as a surprise.

188
Buy tickets to his favorite ball game.

189
Give him a back rub.

190
Hire all or part of the yard work done
for a week or month to give him a nice break
from what he would normally do.

191
Set up a fishing trip for him
and his best friend.

192
Go four wheeling together.

193
Throw the football or baseball with him.

194
Tell him he is your knight in shining armor.

195
Go on a scary ride with him.

196
Study the players of his favorite sport
and talk to him about them.

197
Plan a surprise picnic.

198
Tell him some things you love about him.

199
Buy some of his favorite snack foods,
and prepare a care package
for him to keep at work.

200
Take an evening swim together.

201
Invite his friends over for a ball game.

202
Write a love note
and put it in his suitcase
before he leaves for a trip.

203
Plan a vacation together.

204
Buy him a special pen to use to sign
an important document.

205
Go to a "shoot 'em up" western movie
if your husband likes them, even if you
don't care for them.

206
Have his car professionally detailed.

207
Together set goals for your marriage.

208
Buy him some new clothes and wrap them
as an "unbirthday" surprise.

209
Thank him for just being himself.

210
Sign up for dance lessons.

211
Get him a flashlight
to mount in an area where he needs it most,
like the utility room or garage.

212

Go on a couples retreat together.

◈

213

Plan a trip
to see the autumn leaves turn color.

214
Watch the sun set together.

215
Play in the snow
and have a snowball fight.

216
Buy him his favorite magazine.

217
Plan a hiking trip for a day.

218
Listen to taped lectures
while riding in the car.

219
Put on a CD or cassette tape of slow music
and dance together.

220
Take him to his favorite restaurant.

221
Let him read the paper without interruption.

222

Buy him a Christmas ornament each year that represents one of his interests or hobbies.

223

Compliment him for his efforts when he is reaching toward a new goal.

224
Hide notes for him around the house
where only he will find them.

———————— ◈ ————————

225
Send for a picture of his favorite sports team
or ballplayer.

226
Drive to a scenic spot and enjoy the view.

227
Listen quietly and let him
express his fears.

228
Play a board game together.

229

After or during a rain,
walk through the puddles together
holding hands.

230

Buy him binoculars to use at concerts
and sports events.

231

Before an important day at work,
hold his hand and tell him
that you believe in him
and will be thinking of him
throughout the day.

232

Go to bed when he does.

233
Have a glamour shot taken of yourself
and frame it for him.

234
Buy him a gift certificate
to his favorite lunch spot
and put it in his wallet.

235
On many small pieces of paper
write down all the ways you appreciate him
and put them in a small keepsake box.

236
Take golf lessons
so you can play golf with him.

237
Put his phone number first
on your telephone speed dial.

238
Squeeze fresh orange juice for him.

239
Give him long, loving hugs.

240

Give him coupons to redeem—
one for a back rub,
one for his favorite dinner.

241

Buy him a Christmas tie.

242

Just listen to his stories of the past.

243
Have all of his shoes
polished or repaired.

244
Schedule a complete
physical for him.

245
Spend the day together
at the amusement park.

246
Read together each morning
from a "thought for the day" book.

247
Give him a plaque with the words
"Greatest Husband."

248
Buy him a special apron
to wear when he barbecues.

249
Rent a boat and spend the day
boating and picnicking.

250
Take him out for an early breakfast.

251
Have a date night once a week.

252
Help him find something he has lost,
even after he has quit looking.

253
Sharpen all his pencils, sort his paper clips,
and straighten his desk at home.

254
Help him decorate his office at work.

255
Find old love letters from him
and share them with him.

256
Scrape the ice and snow off his windshield before
he leaves for work.

257
Give him coffee or hot tea in a car mug
as he walks out the door for work.

258

On your early morning walk or jog
stop by the nearest bakery
and bring home his favorite muffin
for breakfast.

259

When out together, squeeze his hand
to let him know that you love him.

260

Support him when a relative discredits him.

261

Make a place for him
to have his own
"junk" bin or drawer.

262

When you are both ready to go to bed,
check all the doors
and turn the lights out yourself.

263

Know his favorite flavor of frozen yogurt
and get some for him.

264
Walk the dog.

265
Surprise him
and wear a new outfit.

266
Go up in a hot air balloon together.

267
Do something extra special
for his parents.

268

Write him a long love note.

269

Make him homemade soup
when he is sick.

270
Say "Thank you."

271
Have a surprise "theme" party for him
when there is no special occasion.

272
Pull the weeds.

273
Go on a horse and carriage ride
through town together.

274
Say "I love you."

275
Pray for him.

276
When you are going to be late,
call and let him know.

277
Change the air conditioning filter.

278
Cook together.

279
Pick up his dirty clothes for him.

280
Have a pillow fight.

281
Call to tell him you love him.

282
Put his shoes away neatly.

283
Send one of his favorite books to the author
to get a personal autograph.

284
Take him to an antique car show.

285

Get a glare screen for his computer
if he spends a lot of time in front of it.

286

Rake the leaves together.

287

Play his favorite music in the house.

288
Buy him bubble gum
when you go to a baseball game.

289
When you are angry with him, express it or deal
with it. Never give him the silent treatment.

290
Say "Excuse me."

291

Order the service manual
for the car he is driving.

292

Replace burned out light bulbs.

293

Lay out his clothes for him.

294
Let him choose the thermostat setting at night.

295
Make him some popcorn
and hot chocolate.

296
Bring him a glass of iced tea or soda
while he is working on a project.

297
Use "I messages" like "I feel angry when. . . ."

298
If you are served a bigger portion
of the same item, trade with him.

299
Wear a piece of jewelry he bought you
that you haven't worn in a while.

300
Encourage him to pursue a hobby.

301
Keep his sock and underwear drawer full.

302
Water the garden and cut some flowers
for the house.

303
Make homemade ice cream together.

304
Clean his workbench.

305
Dress up fifties-style with some friends
and go to a local Sonic or "drive in" restaurant.

306
Buy him new barbecue utensils.

307
Write a letter and send pictures
of your immediate family to his relatives.

308
When eating out, share one meal.

309
Allow him to grieve over his losses.

310
Clip articles from magazines and newspapers
that may be of interest to him.

311
Be accountable to each other.

312
Help him complete a project that is due.

313
Inform him when his favorite clothing store
is having a sale.

314
Attend PTA meetings together.

315

Draw a family tree so he can learn your relatives' names and relationship to one another.

316

Keep your promises.

317

Restate what he has said to you, making sure you understood him.

318

Together learn the meaning of a new word
and see how many times you can use it
during the week.

319

Have a jar to collect his pocket change.

320

Visit his boyhood home.

321
Decorate your house for the various seasons
and holidays.

322
Bake homemade bread for him.

323
Listen to him while he is telling a story.
Never interrupt.

324
Call a radio station and dedicate a song to him.

325
Keep his travel shaving kit well supplied.

326
Put his car seat back in position
after you've driven his car.

327

Go Christmas caroling with a group of couples.

328

Make him a first aid kit for his car.

329

When he is explaining something to you, let him
finish completely before you ask a question
or state your feelings.

330

When it comes time to do something about his favorite chair, talk to him about having it reupholstered, never about throwing it away.

───────── ◈ ─────────

331

Compliment his haircut.

───────── ◈ ─────────

332

Leave his personal mail unopened.

333
Go to a greeting card store together
and enjoy reading and laughing at the cards.

334
Go to a professional conference or meeting
to learn more about his profession.

335
Clean his sunglasses for him.

336

When dashing out to the market or making your weekly shopping list, ask him if there is anything he needs while you are out.

◈

337

Scratch both of your initials in wet cement.

◈

338

Have your blood pressure taken together at the drugstore.

339

When you go out to listen to a band,
request that they play your favorite song.

340

Stock up on his shaving cream, razor blades,
toothpaste, toothbrush, and deodorant.

341

Go to a concert in the park.

342
Make a video of interviews with close friends,
family members, or your children
on how special he is.

343
Ask for his advice.

344
Keep a stash of his favorite candy bars.

345

Organize his side of the closet
and his chest of drawers.

346

Renew your wedding vows to each other with
clergy present. Invite family and friends to watch
the ceremony, then stay for cake and punch.

347

Appreciate the ways he is different from you.

348

Love him even when you don't feel like
loving him.

349

Before you go on vacation, get maps of the areas
you will be visiting for him to look over.

350

Slow the pace by taking a trip together
on the train.

351
Never volunteer him for a job
without asking him first.

352
Remember what he likes on his sandwiches—
i.e., lettuce, tomato, onion, relish, mustard,
mayonnaise, type of bread, etc.

353
Don't expect to understand him completely.

354

Remind him of his mother's birthday.

355

When he returns from work, ask him what was
the nicest thing that was said to him that day.

356

When eating out, order two different entrees
and share them.

357
Take the blame.

358
Share the credit.

359
Let him read uninterrupted in the bathroom
(or his favorite place of choice).

360

When he addresses an audience,
sit in the front row and smile.

361

Accept his suggestions.

362

Wait to recycle the newspaper until you are sure
he is finished with it.

363
Write a book with him.

364
Don't write a book with him.

365
Tell him you love him as often as he can stand it.

The Smallest Caring Act Can Become a Caring Tradition

I give cooking lessons to my daughters, Kari and Laura. When they first started, it was hard for them to understand that a "little packet of yeast" can cause a small ball of bread dough to rise and fill a large bowl with dough. The same can be true for adults who have trouble believing that "little acts of kindness" on a daily basis can bring new life to a marriage. But it's true!

Little acts of kindness mean a lot in a relationship. Clinical studies have shown that when a marriage shows signs of trouble, if the spouses begin doing "little acts of kindness" on a daily basis, it can actually bring back "feelings" of love toward their spouse. For those marriages that are doing well it can be an added source of enrichment.

Sometimes the smallest caring act can become a caring tradition. Perhaps, an annual getaway to the place where he proposed to you or maybe it's a walk along the beach or around your neighborhood. One of our traditions is our date night. We always include dinner out, but after that variety takes place. We cherish this tradition of eating out and spending time alone. We really couldn't do without it.

Another caring tradition has been to have the kids become involved (with the help of a parent) in making a special birthday cake and dinner for Dad or Mom. Decorations and party hats are usually included.

A tradition I hope will be a part of our marriage and family for as long as we live is a special plate that we have in our home. This special plate comes out for one person at dinner when we want to say, "I love you," "Great job," "Congratulations," "Sorry it was a tough day, but we care about you," etc.

In this book, Cay and I have given you 365 ways to express your love for your husband. But don't stop there! Become a student of your husband. What does he like or dislike? Ask him for a list of things that make him feel loved or that he would like you to do for him or with him. Even in using the ideas in this book, the element of surprise can still be there. He doesn't know when or which one you are going to do. Just begin to practice these loving actions and soon they'll become a habit! What's more, they're fun!

For example, when John and I were first married we acquired a little five-inch stuffed lion. We called him Mr. Lion. I am not sure where he came from. He looked quite worn (although his coloring was very much like that of a real lion). And I am sure someone purchased him at a dime store for fifty cents or less. Mr. Lion became Mr. Hide and Seek. John once hid him in the medicine cabinet, and when I opened the door, he fell out and I screamed! I hid Mr. Lion under John's pillow. He hid Mr. Lion in my coat pocket. I stuck Mr. Lion on the steering wheel of John's car. This game went on for months.

Sometimes Mr. Lion wouldn't appear for days and then he'd show up someplace totally unexpected . . . like the freezer! You never knew where or when Mr. Lion would appear, but it was fun and a great surprise. Now I wonder what happened to Mr. Lion. Will I one day look in a box or cabinet that has remained untouched for some time and find him? It was such a small thing, but it's meant so much. . . . Just like it can for you.

—CINDY TRENT

$6.00 U.S.

Sometimes the little things in life can make a big difference. As a wife, you've probably seen how the smallest things can have a huge impact on the way your husband thinks and acts. Although your husband may respond to different *forms* of encouragement than you do, he still wants and needs those expressions of your love. And no one is in a better position to offer love and encouragement to your husband than you.

Need some ideas on how to show your husband just how much you care? *How to Be Your Husband's Best Friend* contains a whole year's worth of ideas to try. It offers 365 simple and creative activities that you can do with or for your husband. You'll be amazed at how small investments can pay such big dividends!

Left: Cay Bolin and her husband, Dan.

Right: Cindy Trent and her husband, John.

PIÑON PRESS

ISBN: 0-89109-874-7

9 780891 098744   50600